What Not To Feed Your Dog

What Not To Feed Your Dog

TONI ILSLEY

Text Toni Ilsley
Copyright © Toni Ilsley

First print October 2024

CONTENTS

CHAPTER 1: FROM TRAGEDY TO TRANSFORMATION: THE ORIGINS OF CHARLIE'S PLACE — 9

CHAPTER 2: FROM WOLVES TO CHIHUAHUAS: THE EVOLUTION OF CANINE DIETS — 21

CHAPTER 3: THE GOOD, THE BAD, AND THE UGLY: DECODING COMMERCIAL DOG FOODS — 29

CHAPTER 4: ALTERNATIVE DIETS: RAISE A PAW IF YOU WANT RAW! — 35

CHAPTER 5: PUPPY POWER TO SEDENTARY SENIOR: NUTRITION THROUGH THE LIFE STAGES — 43

CHAPTER 6: THE ALLERGY PUZZLE: IDENTIFYING AND MANAGING FOOD SENSITIVITIES — 51

CHAPTER 7: TREATS, CHEWS, AND SUPPLEMENTS: ENHANCING YOUR BEST FRIEND'S DIET — 57

CHAPTER 8: THE POOP SCOOP: WHAT YOUR DOG'S WASTE IS TRYING TO TELL YOU!   61

CHAPTER 9: CHOPPERS AND CHOW: DENTAL HEALTH AND NUTRITION   69

CHAPTER 10: BEYOND THE BOWL: EXERCISE, MENTAL STIMULATION, AND HOLISTIC HEALTH   77

CHAPTER 1: FROM TRAGEDY TO TRANSFORMATION: THE ORIGINS OF CHARLIE'S PLACE

Life has a way of taking unexpected turns, sometimes leading us down paths we never could have imagined. My journey into the world of dog care and nutrition began with unimaginable heartbreak, but it has become a source of healing, purpose, and a way to honour the memory of my son, Charlie.

Before my life changed forever, I worked in hospital pharmacy. It was a career I had dedicated 25 years to, and one I thought I would continue until retirement. My days were filled with medications, prescriptions, and the hustle and bustle of hospital life, but little did I know that my expertise in pharmaceuticals would soon be put to a very personal test.

When Charlie was diagnosed with a brain tumour at the age of eight, our world was turned upside down. As a mother, I felt helpless in the face of such a devastating diagnosis, and we threw ourselves into his treatment, determined to fight this battle with everything we had. The journey was gruelling, filled with chemotherapy, radiotherapy, and countless hospital visits, but throughout this challenging time, Charlie had one consistent wish; he wanted a dog.

As many people are, we had always been busy with work, and the timing never seemed quite right for a pet, but now, faced with Charlie's illness, how could we deny him? That's when Eric, a Lhasa Apso, came into our lives, even though his arrival meant that we had defied the doctor's advice against getting a dog during Charlie's treatment due to his weakened immune system. But we did everything we could to make sure Eric would be hypoallergenic and safe for Charlie.

Eric quickly became Charlie's constant companion, offering comfort and unconditional love during the toughest of times, and that dog spent every minute with him, sitting on Charlie's lap while he was learning to get his co-ordination back and play his PlayStation, or just being there for a cuddle.

As Charlie's treatment progressed, we found ourselves travelling the world in search of alternative therapies, and it was during a trip to Mexico for treatment that Charlie's love of dogs truly blossomed. We stayed at a ranch where they rescued all manner of canine companions, and it was here that Charlie had an experience that would leave a lasting impact. There was one dog at that ranch that had had an astonishing 11 puppies, and Charlie, in his wheelchair, looked up at me from amidst this sea of soulful eyes and wagging tails and said, 'Mum, when I grow up, I really want to do this. I want to look after dogs.'

That moment, just three days before we lost Charlie, became the seed that would grow into Charlie's Dog Place. Charlie's words, expressing his dream to work with dogs when he grew up, became a guiding light for me in the dark days that followed his passing and my life changed forever.

After Charlie died, I found myself at a crossroads. The life of a hospital ACT, which had been my world for so long, suddenly felt empty and meaningless. I knew I had to do something to honour Charlie's memory, to make his short life continue to have meaning and impact. I left the hospital knowing that I had to set up Charlie's Place, and although the decision wasn't easy, it felt right. It was as if Charlie had left me a roadmap for my future, a way to channel my grief into something positive, something that would help others too, whether they had four legs or two.

Starting Charlie's Dog Place was a leap into the unknown as I had no experience running a business, let alone one centred around dog care, but I had determination, love for Charlie's memory, and a growing passion for dogs that surprised even me.

The early days were challenging, to say the least. I started the business from my home, which quickly proved to be less than ideal as the dogs were trashing the place - the garden, the house, everything – and not only was my home being overrun by enthusiastic canines, I also found myself in an awkward position with potential clients. People were coming to look around and staying in my kitchen for an hour at a time, which was starting to blur the boundaries between my personal and professional life.

Moreover, running the business from home was taking an emotional toll as I was still grieving deeply for Charlie, so it was clear that I needed to find a dedicated space for the business to grow and for me to heal.

Fortune smiled on me when I heard about a doggy daycare facility that was closing down in Sonning Common. The owner was leaving for Switzerland and offered to sell me the business, including a van, for just a pound! It was an opportunity I couldn't pass up, even though the place was, frankly, a rundown mess.

Taking over this facility was a significant step forward. We started with 18 dogs, combining the 12 from the existing business with the six I had been caring for at home, and it wasn't easy - the place needed a lot of work to bring it up to standard, and I had to borrow money to make the necessary improvements - but it was a start, a really hopeful, positive beginning for Charlie's Dog Place.

From those humble beginnings, the business has grown beyond my wildest expectations. Today, we care for about 100 dogs a week, offering daycare, boarding, and grooming services, and I've been able to employ five amazing people, creating a team that shares my passion for dog care.

But running a successful dog care business isn't just about loving dogs; it requires knowledge, skills, and continuous learning, so I threw myself into education, determined to provide the best possible care for the dogs entrusted to us. I started with a first aid course, then moved on to dog training and behaviour courses, and my thirst for knowledge didn't stop there! I'm currently pursuing a master's degree in dog training, constantly expanding my understanding of canine behaviour and needs.

One area that particularly captured my interest was dog nutrition. As I spent more time around dogs and their humans, I began to realise how little I - and many others - knew about what we were really feeding our best friends. I was shocked by the amount of rubbish that goes into many commercial dog foods, and this realisation sparked a passion for learning about canine nutrition that has become a core part of my mission at Charlie's Dog Place.

The more I learned, the more shocked I became at the ingredients in many commercial dog foods. It wasn't just the poor quality of ingredients that concerned me, but also the lack of awareness among dog parents. Many people, like myself before I started this journey, simply didn't know what they were feeding their dogs or the potential health implications.

This lack of education about dog nutrition became a driving force and I felt that by sharing my knowledge, I could help improve the lives of dogs beyond just those in my care at Charlie's Dog Place. It became another way to honour Charlie's memory; by helping the dogs he loved so much.

Running Charlie's Dog Place has been more than just a business venture or a career change. It has been a journey of healing, of finding purpose in the wake of unimaginable loss, and I think the dogs have helped me as much as I've learned to help them. Every day brings new challenges and rewards. From dealing with difficult behaviours to celebrating the progress of a nervous dog, each experience adds to my understanding and passion for this work.

The transformation from hospital pharmacist to dog care expert has been profound. My house is now filled with books on dogs, certificates from various courses, and a constant drive to learn more. I won't ever stop learning about these amazing animals.

This journey, born from tragedy, has become a testament to the healing power of purpose and the unexpected ways life can guide us. Charlie's wish to work with dogs when he grew up has become my reality, a way to keep his spirit alive and to make a positive impact in the world he left too soon.

Charlie's Dog Place is more than just a business. It's a living, breathing tribute to a little boy who loved dogs, a place where his spirit lives on in every wagging tail and happy bark, and through this work, I've found a way to transform my grief into something therapeutic, to create joy from sorrow, and to keep learning and growing every day.

As I continue on this path, educating dog parents about proper nutrition and care, expanding our services, and always striving to provide the best possible environment for our canine clients, I know that Charlie would be proud that his short life continues to have a profound impact, touching the lives of hundreds of dogs and their humans.

In the end, this journey has taught me that sometimes our greatest purpose can emerge from our deepest pain. Charlie's dream of working with dogs has become my reality, and through it, I've found healing, purpose, and a way to keep his memory alive. As I look to the future, I'm excited to continue learning, growing, and honouring Charlie's legacy through the work we do at Charlie's Dog Place. In this book, I hope you too find new ways to show your furry friend how much you love them.

My Charlie

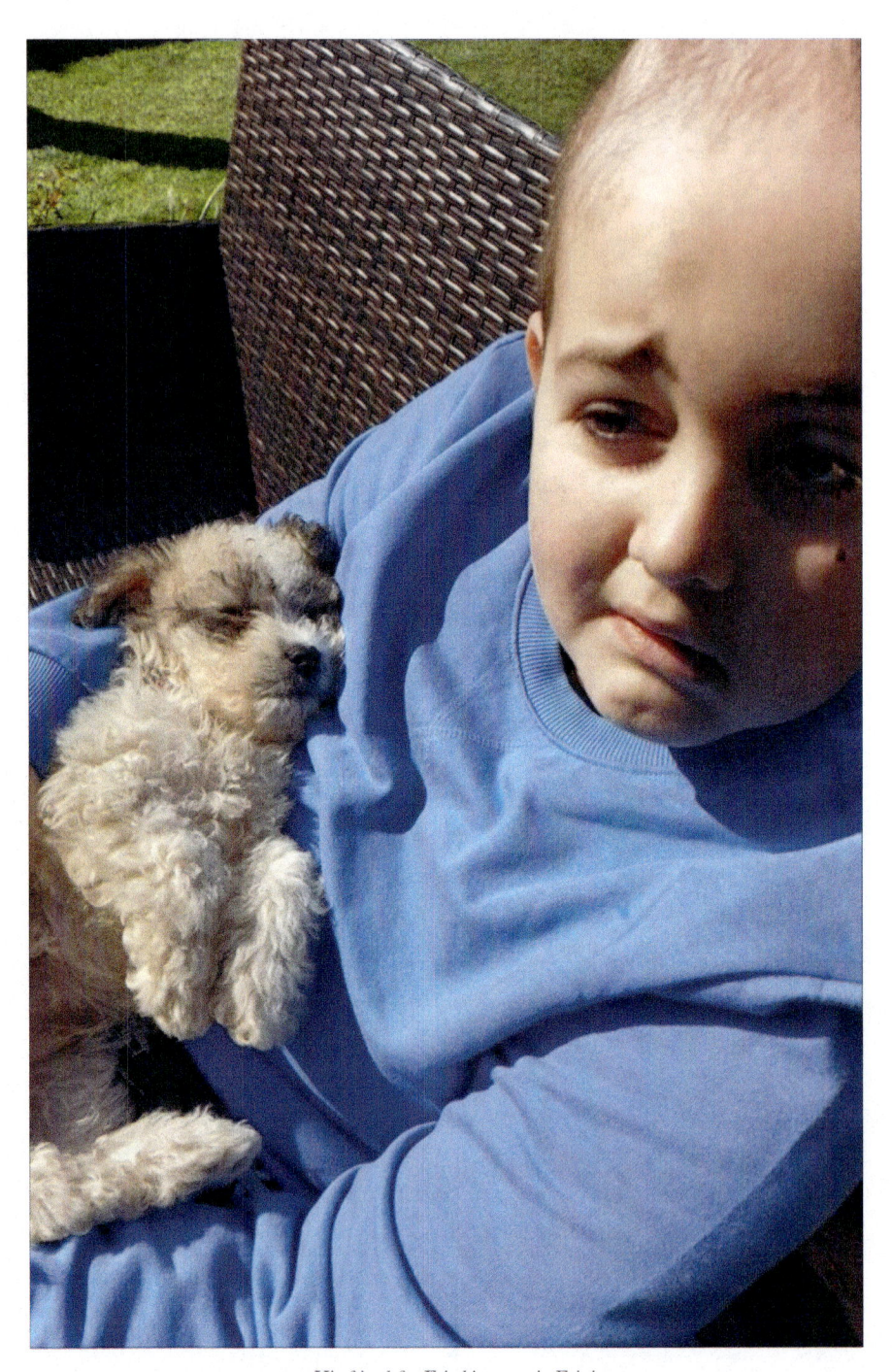

His friend for Eric his name is Erinie

His best friend Eric

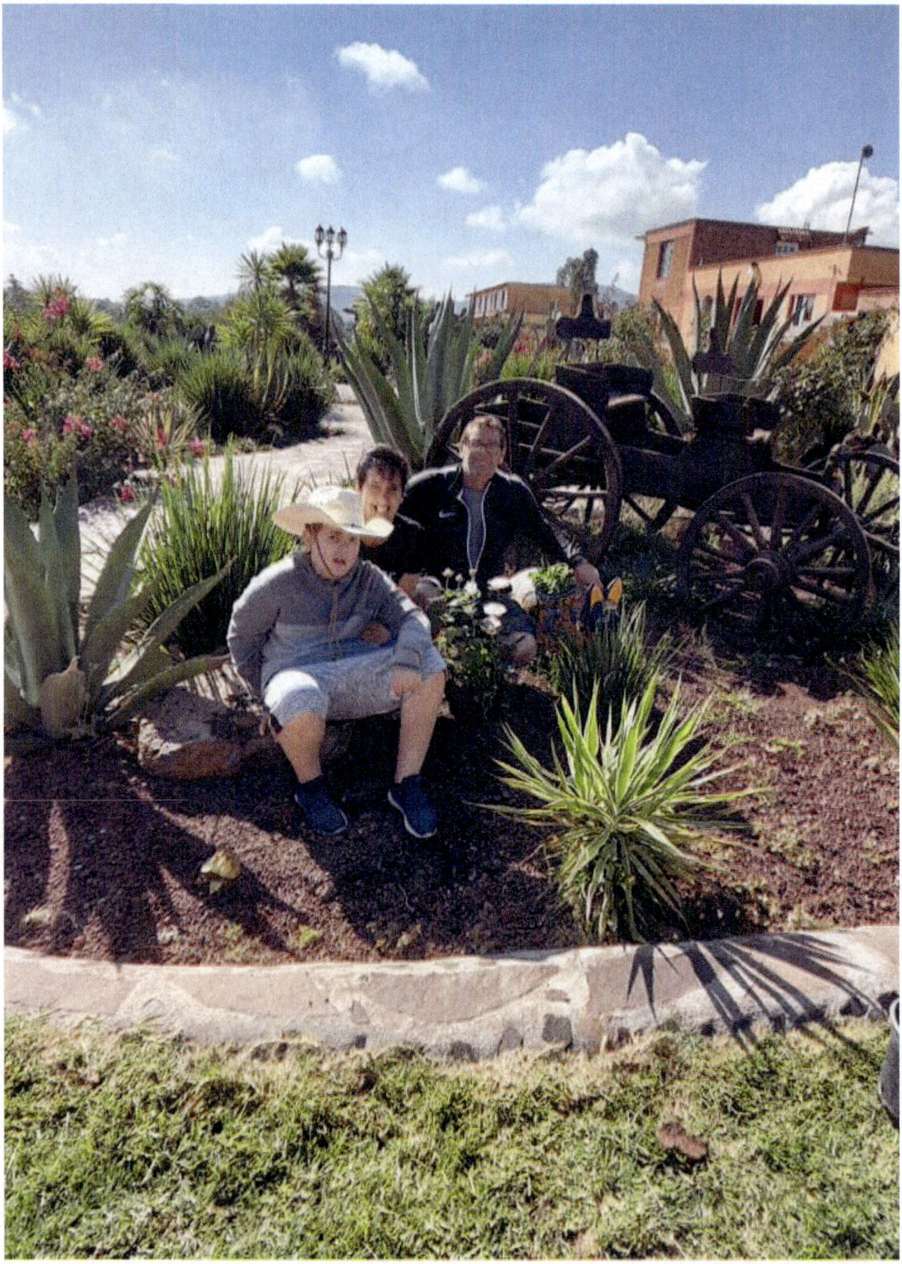

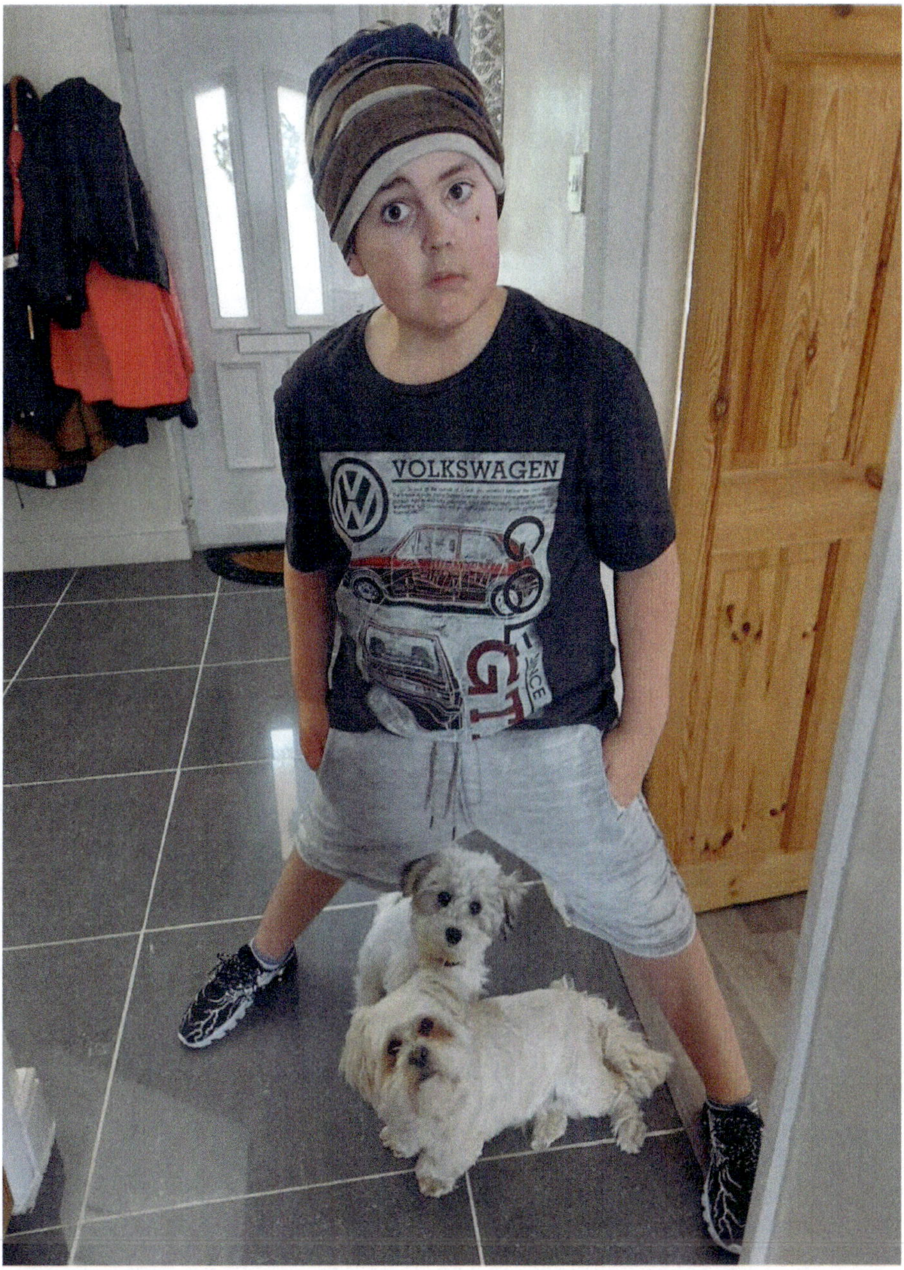
VOLKSWAGEN

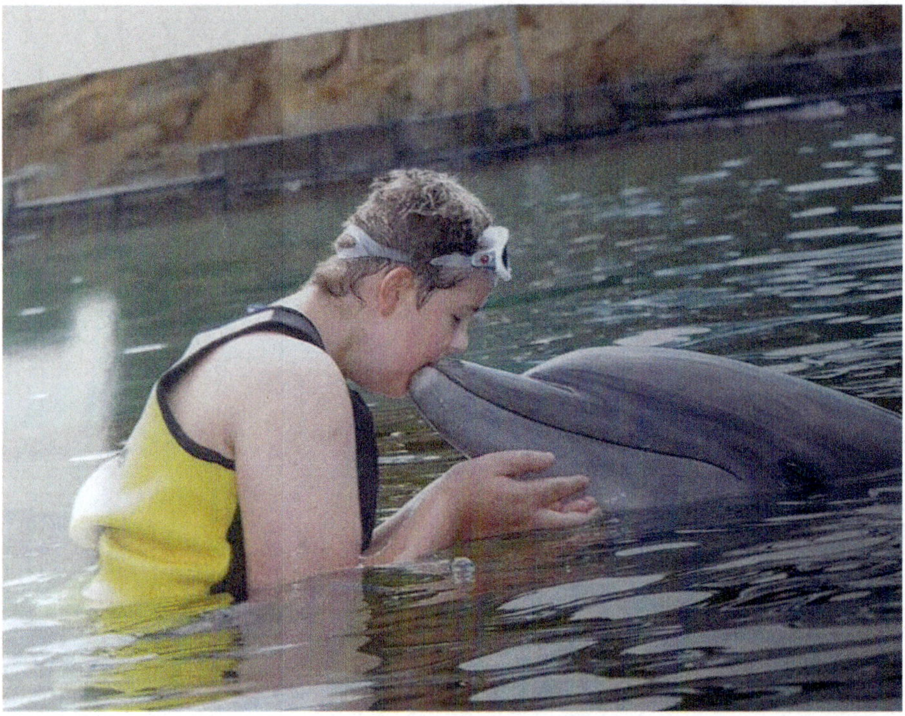

CHAPTER 2: FROM WOLVES TO CHIHUAHUAS: THE EVOLUTION OF CANINE DIETS

I've become captivated by the incredible evolutionary journey of man's best friend. As a dog lover who now runs a doggy daycare and consults on canine nutrition and behaviour, I've developed a deep fascination with how our beloved four-legged companions have changed over time. It's mind-boggling to think that the adorable, cheeky Chihuahua or the playful little Dachshund shares a common ancestor with the majestic grey wolf!

The story of how dogs became domesticated began many thousands of years ago, and while there is still some debate amongst experts about the exact timelines, recent evidence suggests that the process may have started even before the Last Glacial Period, which occurred between 20,000 to 30,000 years ago. As nomadic humans began forming the first settlements, the most curious and confident wolves likely started hanging around the outskirts, perhaps attracted by the tantalising smells of the hunters' fresh kills.

Over time, a mutually beneficial relationship developed. The wolves learned that if they approached the humans' campfires, they might get tossed some tasty scraps, and in return, their presence provided a level of protection, deterring other predators from raiding the camps. The canines' superior senses and tracking abilities also made them useful hunting partners.

To understand how today's dogs' dietary needs have changed, it's helpful to examine the eating habits of these wild ancestors, as the natural wolf diet consists primarily of meat, bones, and the vegetation found in the stomachs of their prey animals. As hunters, they are adapted to eat huge amounts of food at a time when a kill is made, sometimes as much as 20 pounds in a single meal! Their powerful jaws exert around 400 pounds of pressure per square inch, compared to about 320 for a large domestic dog, and a mere 120 for the average human. After gorging, a wolf pack may go several days without eating again as they sleep off their feast.

As the generations passed and wolves evolved into the first dogs, their digestive systems gradually adapted to accommodate the new foods their human companions offered. I found it fascinating to learn that dogs today produce significantly more digestive enzymes in their saliva compared to wolves, and this adaptation allows them to begin breaking down the complex carbohydrates found in many commercial diets. Wolves' saliva lacks this ability.

It's a common assumption that huskies, with their wolf-like appearance, are the most closely related to their wild cousins, however, genetic testing has revealed a surprising fact: the small, fluffy, insanely cute Shih Tzu actually has the most similar DNA! This speaks to the incredible physical diversity that developed as humans selectively bred dogs to suit different purposes.

Speaking of Shih Tzus, here is another incredible fact that highlights just how much dogs have changed: all breeds are still so genetically similar despite their appearances that a massive Great Dane can produce viable offspring with a tiny Shih Tzu. As long as the Great Dane is the mother, such a mismatched pairing could result in a litter of incredibly unique mixed-breed pups; although I would probably not recommend it!

In the early days of domestication, dogs served exclusively as working animals. Various jobs included guarding livestock and homes, herding sheep, and assisting on hunts. It wasn't until much later that the idea of keeping a dog solely as a pet companion arose and selective breeding for looks and temperament became common practice.

The establishment of kennel clubs in the Victorian era sparked the development of formal breed standards, which is why we now have so many distinct types of dogs, and some breeds' original purposes have had a fascinating impact on their physical characteristics. Beagles, for example, were favoured as hunting hounds for their phenomenal sense of smell, and breeders took advantage of the trait by intentionally selecting for large, wide noses and long, floppy ears.

The hounds' giant ears serve an important purpose on the hunting trail for as the dog runs, the ears sweep the ground, collecting odour particles and wafting them up into the vicinity of the nose. The extra surface area provides a wider net for capturing faint scents, and the droopy ears also trap the smells around the face so the Beagle can make the most of every clue.

Another interesting bit of canine trivia: while dogs can see colours, their spectrum of visible light is limited compared to ours. They can detect blue and yellow hues, but reds and greens tend to look greyish. This means that when choosing toys and training tools, blue and yellow items will be the most visually stimulating to our furry friends!

Though we may refer to a juicy steak as a 'mouth-watering' treat, the truth is that the way dogs experience food is quite different from us. While humans have about 9,000 taste buds, dogs have only around 1,700, and their eating decisions are driven almost entirely by their super-powered sense of smell. Dogs also have special taste buds dedicated just to tasting water, something humans lack entirely!

As people have grown more health-conscious about their own diets, many have started to question the ingredients in commercial dog foods as well. A growing number of dog lovers, myself included, have transitioned their pets to a raw diet centred around meaty bones, aiming to mimic the ancestral diet of their wolf predecessors.

Though dogs have evolved to coexist with humans in an impressive array of shapes, sizes and personalities, we can still honour their inner wolf by recognizing their instinctive nutritional needs. By taking a cue from the raw, prey-based diet that sustained their ancestors for millennia, perhaps we can help our beloved companions live the happiest, healthiest lives possible in the modern era. As we've seen, every breed

WHAT NOT TO FEED YOUR DOG

from the Chihuahua to the Great Dane is just a wolf in dog's clothing!

Sansa the chihuahua

Atlas the husky

CHAPTER 3: THE GOOD, THE BAD, AND THE UGLY: DECODING COMMERCIAL DOG FOODS

The world of commercial dog food is far more complex than most pet owners realise, and what we see on the shelves of our local supermarkets often masks a disturbing reality about what we're actually feeding our beloved canine companions. This chapter aims to shed light on the ingredients, labelling practices, and how to differentiate between high-quality and low-quality options in the vast sea of commercial dog foods.

Many foods contain questionable ingredients that would shock most pet owners if they knew the truth, but perhaps the most disturbing of these are the 'meat derivatives'. This innocuous-sounding term can include some truly horrifying ingredients: euthanised pets, roadkill, and diseased animals, to name but a few examples of what might be lurking in your dog's food bowl under the guise of 'meat derivatives'. It's a sobering thought that the pets we love and care for could end up as food for other dogs after they've passed away...

But it doesn't stop there. Some dog foods contain a form of antifreeze to retain moisture content. Yes, you read that correctly; a substance that's toxic to dogs in its pure form is being used as a food additive, and it's practices like these that highlight the need for pet owners to be vigilant about what they're feeding their dogs.

When examining popular brands, you might be surprised to learn that many contain very little actual meat. I've encountered foods where the meat content is as low as 4%, with the rest being made up of cereals, grains, and nutritionally deficient fillers, which is particularly concerning when you consider that dogs are primarily carnivores, and their bodies are designed to digest and utilise meat proteins efficiently.

So, what should we be looking for in a high-quality dog food? First and foremost, the first ingredient should be meat, ideally at least 50-70%. When reading the ingredient list, be wary of cereals, maize, and other fillers, as these ingredients have little nutritional value for dogs and are often used simply to bulk out the food and make it cheaper to produce.

Some cheaper foods use vegetable derivatives, which often consist of stalks, cores, and other parts of vegetables that aren't particularly nutritious, and while vegetables can be beneficial for dogs in the right quantities, these particular derivatives offer little in terms of nutritional value.

Another ingredient to watch out for is pea protein. Recent studies have shown a link between pea protein and cardiac problems in dogs, and it's often used as a cheaper alternative to meat protein, but is not an ideal source of nutrition for our canine friends. When examining dog food labels, look for named meat sources rather than generic terms like 'meat meal'. 'Chicken', 'beef', or 'lamb' are much more transparent than vague terms that could encompass a wide range of animal products. It's also crucial to avoid foods with artificial colours, sweeteners, and preservatives as these additives serve no nutritional purpose and can potentially cause behavioural issues and other health problems in dogs.

You might think that foods recommended by vets would be safe from these issues, but unfortunately, that's not always the case and some vet-recommended foods may not be ideal. Vets often receive a percentage of sales for recommending certain brands, which can influence their recommendations, although this doesn't mean they're intentionally trying to harm our pets, just that they might not have the most up-to-date information on canine nutrition.

When it comes to wet foods, quality can vary greatly. Many tinned foods contain jelly-like substances of questionable origin that don't offer much in terms of nutrition, and although they might smell appealing to dogs, they often don't provide the balanced diet our pets deserve.

It's important to note that expensive foods are not always better. Some premium-priced foods are no better nutritionally than their cheaper counterparts, so it's crucial to research the ingredients before spending your hard-earned money! Don't be swayed by fancy packaging or high prices; the true measure of a dog food's quality is in its ingredients.

One of the biggest challenges we face as consumers is the vague labelling of pet food ingredients, and legal loopholes allow manufacturers to be less than transparent about what's actually in the food. For example, they might list 'meat and animal derivatives' without specifying what animals those derivatives come from, and this lack of transparency makes it difficult for pet owners to make informed decisions about what they're feeding their dogs.

The impact of poor-quality dog food goes beyond just nutrition. Food additives in particular can potentially cause behavioural issues and other problems in dogs, and I've seen cases where changing a dog's diet has led to improvements in everything from energy levels to anxiety. It's a stark reminder of how closely linked diet is to overall health and wellbeing in our canine companions.

In conclusion, navigating the world of commercial dog foods can be challenging, but it's a challenge worth taking on for the health and happiness of our pets, and by understanding what to look for and what to avoid, we can make informed decisions about what we feed our dogs. Remember, our dogs rely on us for their nutrition. They can't read labels or make informed choices about what they eat, so that responsibility falls to us, and it's one we should take seriously. After all, good nutrition is the foundation of good health, and don't our loyal companions deserve the very best we can give them?

What not to feed your dog cheap kibble

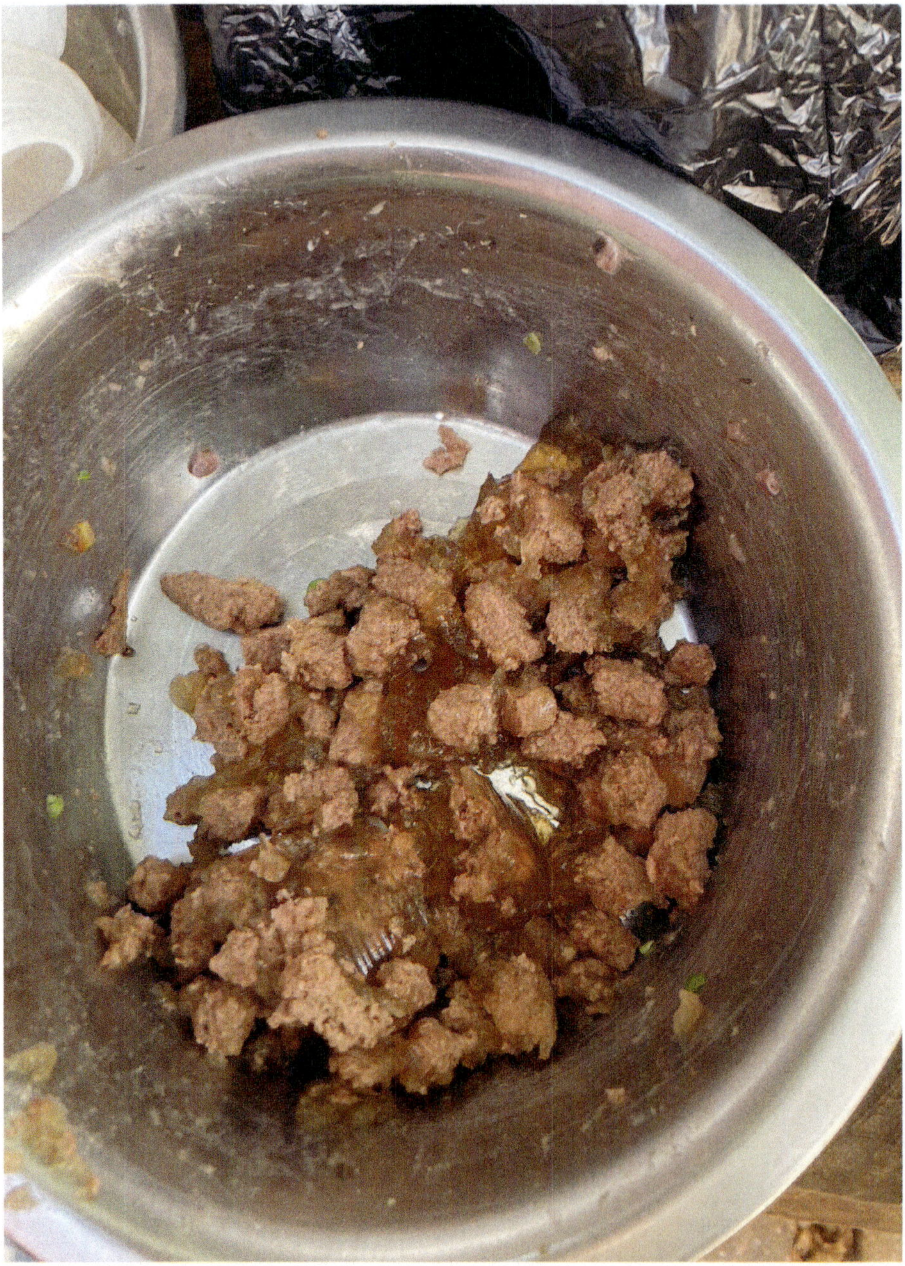

CHAPTER 4: ALTERNATIVE DIETS: RAISE A PAW IF YOU WANT RAW!

The world of dog nutrition has evolved significantly in recent years, with many pet owners looking beyond standard commercial dog foods to alternative options that promise better health and vitality for their furry friends. This chapter explores these alternatives, focusing on raw diets, home-prepared meals, and the option of mixing different types of food.

Raw diets have been gaining popularity among dog owners, driven by the desire to provide a more natural, ancestral diet for our canine companions. The concept is simple: mimic the diet of wolves, the ancestors of our domestic dogs. This approach assumes that dogs' digestive systems are still best suited to the kind of food their wild cousins eat.

One raw food option that has gained traction is Nature's Menu, which comes in convenient frozen cubes, making it easy to portion and store. These cubes contain a mix of meat, vegetables, and fruits like cranberries, with meat making up about 80 percent of the content, and this balance aims to provide a nutritionally complete meal that's close to what a dog might eat in the wild.

The benefits of raw diets can be quite remarkable. Many dog owners report improvements in coat condition, energy levels, and even stool quality after switching to raw. Dogs often become more enthusiastic about mealtimes, and some owners notice a reduction in allergies or skin problems.

However, it's crucial to understand that raw diets aren't without risks. The potential for bacterial contamination is a significant concern. Salmonella and E. coli are common bacteria found in raw meat that can be harmful to both dogs and humans, so to minimize this risk, it's essential to practice proper food handling and storage. Always wash your hands thoroughly after handling raw meat, use separate utensils and a separate preparation area for your dog's food, and never leave raw food sitting out at room temperature. Frozen raw food should be thawed in the refrigerator, not on the counter.

Another concern with raw diets is ensuring nutritional balance. It's not as simple as just feeding your dog raw meat. A balanced raw diet should include the right proportions of muscle meat, organ meat, and bone, as well as some plant matter. This is why consulting with a vet or canine nutritionist before making the switch is highly recommended, so that they can help you design a diet that meets all of your dog's nutritional needs.

One of the most noticeable benefits of raw feeding that I've observed is improved stool quality. It might not be the most pleasant topic, but any dog owner knows that what comes out of their dog is a good indicator of what's going on inside. Raw-fed dogs often have smaller, firmer stools that are easier to pick up - a definite plus for any dog owner! As I often tell clients, raw-fed dogs have 'pretty good poos' and that's happy days for both dogs and humans who don't like vet bills!

Home-prepared meals are another alternative that's gaining popularity. The main appeal of home-prepared diets is the control it gives owners over their dog's nutrition. You know exactly what's going into your dog's food bowl; no mystery meat, no questionable by-products, just wholesome ingredients that you've chosen yourself.

Variety is key in home-prepared diets. Just as we wouldn't want to eat the same meal every day, dogs benefit from a range of different foods. This not only keeps meals interesting for your dog but also ensures they're getting a wide range of nutrients. You might rotate between different protein sources; chicken one day, beef another, fish on the third, and include a variety of vegetables and healthy carbohydrates.

Many dog owners find a middle ground by mixing commercial food with home-prepared ingredients, and this approach allows you to boost the nutritional value of your dog's diet without the complexity of preparing everything from scratch. For example, you might use a high-quality kibble as a base and add some fresh ingredients on top.

When it comes to adding fresh ingredients, there are plenty of healthy options to choose from. Carrots and apples make great low-calorie treats that most dogs love, and these can be given as stand-alone treats or mixed into meals for added nutrition and variety.

For dogs with digestive issues, sweet potato can be a great option as it's easy on the stomach and packed with nutrients, and adding some mashed sweet potato to a dog's diet has even been known to make a significant difference in managing diarrhoea.

WHAT NOT TO FEED YOUR DOG

If you're looking for high-quality commercial options to mix with home-prepared ingredients, there are some good choices out there. Canagan and Lily's Kitchen are two brands that often receive positive reviews, and Canagan, in particular, is known for its high meat content and grain-free formulas, making it a good choice for dogs with grain sensitivities. Lily's Kitchen, on the other hand, is often recommended as a good mid-range option that offers quality ingredients without breaking the bank.

Regardless of which alternative diet you choose, it's crucial to make the transition gradually. A sudden change can upset your dog's digestive system, leading to vomiting or diarrhoea, so start by mixing a small amount of the new food with your dog's current food. A good rule of thumb is to begin with 25% new food and 75% old food, then over the course of a week or two, gradually increase the proportion of new food while decreasing the old.

Cost is a consideration for many dog owners when it comes to alternative diets and raw and home-prepared diets can be more expensive than commercial kibble, especially if you're using high-quality ingredients, however, it's worth considering that feeding a better-quality diet might save you money on vet bills in the long run. Many owners report fewer health issues and reduced need for veterinary interventions after switching to a higher quality diet.

Raw meat needs to be stored properly to prevent bacterial growth, and home-prepared meals often have a shorter shelf life than commercial kibble, so if you're going the raw route, you'll need enough freezer space to store batches of food. For home-prepared meals, consider cooking in batches and freezing portions for convenience, and always thaw frozen food in the refrigerator, never at room temperature.

It's worth noting that dogs on home-prepared or raw diets may need certain supplements to ensure they're getting all the nutrients they need. Calcium is a common one, especially if you're not feeding whole bones, and the calcium to phosphorus ratio is crucial in a dog's diet, which can be challenging to achieve without supplementation in home-prepared meals. Fish oil is another supplement that can be beneficial, providing essential omega-3 fatty acids which support coat health, joint function, and overall inflammation levels in the body.

Other supplements that might be necessary include vitamin E, which acts as an antioxidant and helps in the absorption of fatty acids, and a vitamin B complex, which supports various bodily functions including metabolism and nerve health. Some dogs might also benefit from probiotics, which support digestive health, but again, this is where consultation with a vet or canine nutritionist is crucial.

One aspect of raw feeding that often gets overlooked is the mental stimulation it can provide. Feeding raw meaty bones or whole prey model diets (where the dog is given whole animals or animal parts) can give your dog a chance to use their natural chewing and problem-solving instincts. This can be particularly beneficial for dogs that get bored easily or have a lot of energy to burn.

I want to emphasise that while raw diets can offer numerous benefits, they're not a magic bullet. Like any approach to feeding, raw diets require careful planning and management to ensure they're meeting all of your dog's nutritional needs. If you're considering making the switch to raw, it's crucial to do your research and, ideally, consult with a veterinarian or canine nutritionist who's knowledgeable about raw feeding. They can help you design a diet that's appropriate for your dog's age, size, and health status, and guide you through the transition process.

Remember, the goal of any feeding approach should be to support your dog's health and wellbeing. Whether that's through a raw diet, high-quality kibble, home-cooked meals, or a combination approach will depend on your individual dog and circumstances.

In my experience, many dogs thrive on raw diets. The improvements I've seen in coat condition, energy levels, dental health, and overall vitality can be remarkable, but what's most rewarding is seeing the joy that healthy, energetic dogs bring to their owners' lives. Whether you're opting for raw, home-prepared, or a mix of commercial and fresh foods, the key is making informed decisions based on your dog's individual needs. Consult with professionals, transition gradually, and monitor your dog's health closely. Your dog will thank you.

I adore raw

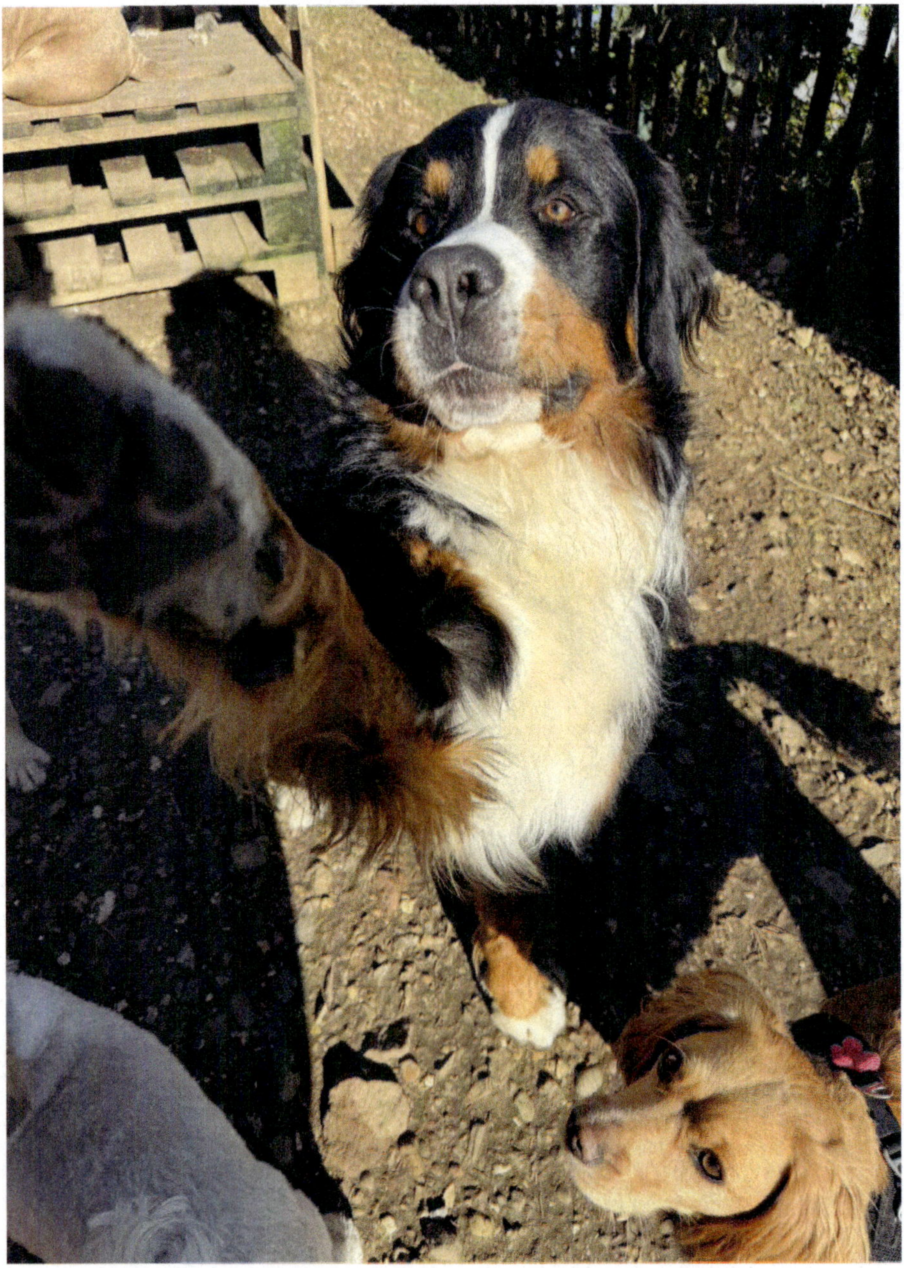

CHAPTER 5: PUPPY POWER TO SEDENTARY SENIOR: NUTRITION THROUGH THE LIFE STAGES

The journey of a dog's life is a remarkable one, filled with changes, growth, and transitions. Just as our nutritional needs change as we progress from infancy to old age, so too do the dietary requirements of our canine companions. In this chapter, we'll explore the fascinating world of canine nutrition through the various life stages, from energetic puppyhood to the golden years of a senior dog.

Let's start at the beginning: the puppy stage. Puppies are bundles of energy, growing at an astounding rate, and their nutritional needs reflect this rapid growth and high energy expenditure. Puppies require a diet that's significantly higher in protein compared to adult dogs, and this high protein content is crucial for supporting their rapid muscle development, bone growth, and overall physical maturation.

I remember when I first brought Eric home. He was a tiny ball of fur, but his appetite was enormous! Puppies like Eric need frequent meals to fuel their growth and keep their energy levels stable, so it's generally recommended to feed puppies three meals a day which helps to support their rapid growth and development.

The protein content in puppy food isn't just higher, it's also of a different quality, and puppy foods are formulated with easily digestible proteins that their developing digestive systems can process efficiently which is why it's so important to feed puppies a diet specifically formulated for their life stage.

Around the age of four to six months for small breeds, or up to 18 months for large breeds, puppies start to transition to an adult feeding schedule which usually means reducing from three meals a day to two. But it's important to make this transition gradually to avoid digestive upset.

Now, let's talk about working dogs. These high-energy canines have unique nutritional requirements that set them apart from the average pet. Working dogs, whether they're herding sheep, assisting in search and rescue operations, or participating in agility competitions, expend a tremendous amount of energy in their daily activities. As a result, they often require a diet that's not only higher in protein but also higher in calories overall.

I've worked with several working dogs, and the difference in their dietary needs compared to pet dogs is striking. These dogs benefit from diets that are not only high in protein but also rich in healthy fats, as the protein supports their muscle development and repair, while the fats provide a concentrated source of energy to fuel their intense activities.

As dogs transition into adulthood, their nutritional needs stabilise, but that doesn't mean their diet becomes any less important. Adult dogs require a balanced diet that maintains their health and energy levels without promoting excessive weight gain, and although the protein content in adult dog food is generally lower, it's still a crucial component of their diet.

One of the most significant changes in a dog's life that can affect their nutritional needs is neutering or spaying. After this procedure, a dog's metabolism often slows down, so I always advise owners to reduce their dog's food intake by about 10% which helps to prevent obesity. Obesity in dogs can lead to a host of health problems, including joint issues, diabetes, and heart disease, so maintaining a healthy weight from puppyhood through to the senior years is vital.

As dogs enter their senior years, their nutritional needs change once again and contrary to what some might expect, senior dogs often need more protein, not less. This is because as dogs age, they tend to lose muscle mass so a higher protein diet can help to keep senior dogs stronger and more mobile.

I've seen the difference a proper senior diet can make firsthand with my own dogs. When Eric entered his senior years, I transitioned him to a diet higher in protein and supplemented with glucosamine and chondroitin, supplements that are crucial for maintaining joint health in older dogs. The change in his energy levels was clear.

Glucosamine and chondroitin can also help to reduce inflammation and many senior dog foods include these supplements, but if not, they can be added separately under the guidance of a vet.

Another crucial aspect of senior dog nutrition is dental health. As dogs age, they become more prone to dental issues, which can affect their ability to eat comfortably, so soft foods or kibble softened with warm water can be easier if they have dental problems. However, it's important to maintain good dental hygiene throughout a dog's life to prevent these issues in the first place.

Small breeds have some unique dietary considerations due to their higher metabolic rates, and need more calories per pound of body weight than larger breeds. They also tend to reach maturity faster, which means they transition to adult food earlier than large breeds, and their small size also means they're more prone to dental issues, so dental health should be a priority from an early age.

One aspect of feeding that remains constant throughout a dog's life is the importance of a consistent feeding schedule. Many owners make the mistake of leaving food out all day for their dogs to graze on, but this practice can lead to overeating and obesity. Set meal times not only help with weight management but also aid in house training puppies and maintaining a routine that dogs find comforting.

Consistent feeding schedules are beneficial for several reasons. Firstly, they help regulate your dog's digestive system, making bathroom habits more predictable, and secondly, scheduled meals allow you to monitor your dog's appetite more closely as a loss of appetite can be an early sign of illness. Lastly, having set meal times helps establish you as the provider of food, which can reinforce your role as the leader in your dog's eyes.

The key to successful feeding throughout a dog's life is awareness and adaptability. This might mean switching to a senior formula as our dogs age, adding supplements as recommended by a vet, or simply adjusting portion sizes to maintain a healthy weight, but remember, every dog is an individual and there will always be exceptions. Always consult with a veterinarian or a canine nutritionist if you're unsure about your dog's specific nutritional needs.

From playful puppies to dignified seniors; by understanding changing needs, we can give our canine companions the best possible chance at a long, healthy, and happy life. After all, they give us their unconditional love; the least we can do is give them the gift of good health through proper nutrition.

The decision was made

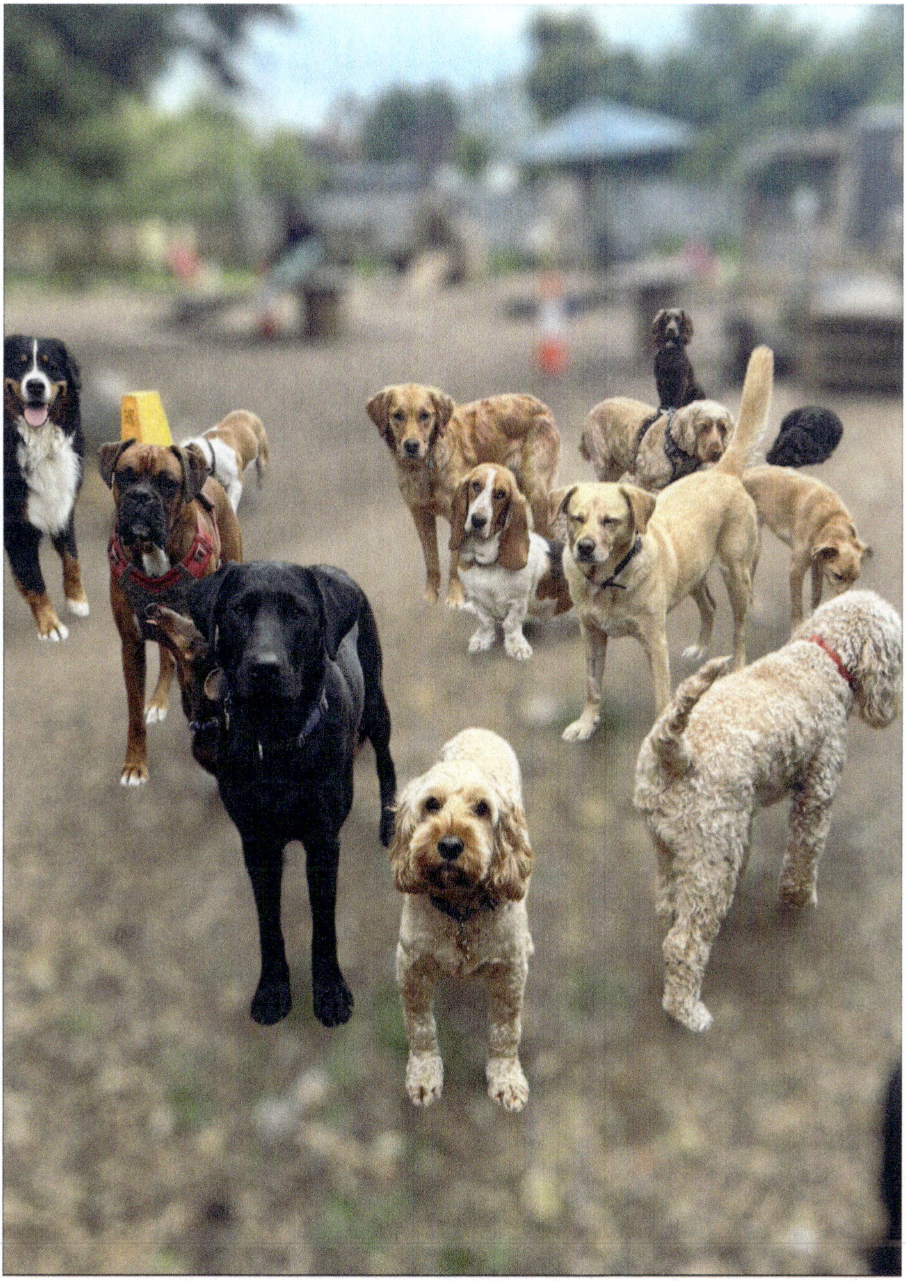

CHAPTER 6: THE ALLERGY PUZZLE: IDENTIFYING AND MANAGING FOOD SENSITIVITIES

Working with dogs at Charlie's Place and through my ongoing research into canine nutrition, I've encountered numerous health issues, but few are as perplexing and frustrating for owners as food allergies and sensitivities. My experience and recent studies have shed new light on this complex topic, and I'm excited to share this information with you.

Let's start with a surprising fact: chicken, that staple of many dog foods, is actually the most common food allergen for dogs. This revelation came as a shock to me, as I'd always considered chicken to be a safe, lean protein source for dogs, but as I've learned, our canine friends can develop allergies to even the most common ingredients in their diets.

Following closely behind chicken is beef, which made me reflect on the many commercial dog foods that rely heavily on these two protein sources. It's no wonder that we're seeing an increase in food allergies among our furry friends.

Now, here's something that might surprise you: wheat isn't necessarily as problematic as we've been led to believe. It's not as common an allergen as chicken or beef, which suggests that we might need to rethink some of our assumptions about canine nutrition.

If a dog is allergic to one protein source, they may also be allergic to others due to similarities in the protein structures, so for example, if a dog is allergic to chicken, they may also react to beef. This information is crucial for managing allergies effectively.

The concept of protein crossovers extends beyond just meat proteins and surprisingly, even rice can sometimes cross-react with chicken allergies. This was a real eye-opener for me, as rice is often considered a safe, easily digestible carbohydrate for dogs, but it just goes to show how complex food allergies can be.

Fish allergies present another interesting case. If a dog is allergic to salmon, for instance, they may well be allergic to other types of fish too, so this is important to keep in mind when trying to find alternative protein sources for allergic dogs.

Given all these potential crossovers, what can we offer? Lamb seems to be a potentially safer option as it appears to have fewer crossover reactions with other proteins, however, as with any dietary change, it's important to introduce new foods gradually and monitor your dog closely for any reactions.

But how do we know if our dogs are suffering from food allergies? The symptoms can be varied, but skin issues are one of the most common signs as dogs with food allergies often have itchy, inflamed skin, and may develop hot spots or excessive scratching. Problems with a dog's coat, such as dullness or excessive shedding, can also be indicators.

Given the complexity of food allergies, reading ingredient lists carefully becomes crucial for being aware of all the components in our dogs' food and how they might interact. I'm used to scrutinizing labels and understanding complex interactions, and I apply these skills to decoding dog food labels too.

Another important consideration is the potential link between pea protein and cardiac issues in dogs, and recent studies have suggested a potential link between diets high in this protein and a type of heart disease called dilated cardiomyopathy (DCM). Also, in some cases, yeast build-up or infections can be related to food allergies and some dogs may be more prone to yeast overgrowth, particularly in their ears or on their skin. This can lead to infections, creating a vicious cycle of inflammation and discomfort.

In some extreme cases, dogs can be allergic to all meat proteins and this presents a significant challenge for feeding, however, there are solutions even for these complex cases. One option that's gaining traction is the use of insect protein, often derived from crickets or mealworms, which provides a novel protein source that most dogs haven't been exposed to before, reducing the likelihood of an allergic reaction.

While the information I've shared here can help you understand the complexities of the issue, diagnosing and managing food allergies often requires professional guidance. The world of canine nutrition is complex and fascinating, much like the dogs we care for, and as we continue to learn more about food allergies and sensitivities in dogs, we're better equipped to provide our furry friends with the nutrition they need to thrive.

Sore ears

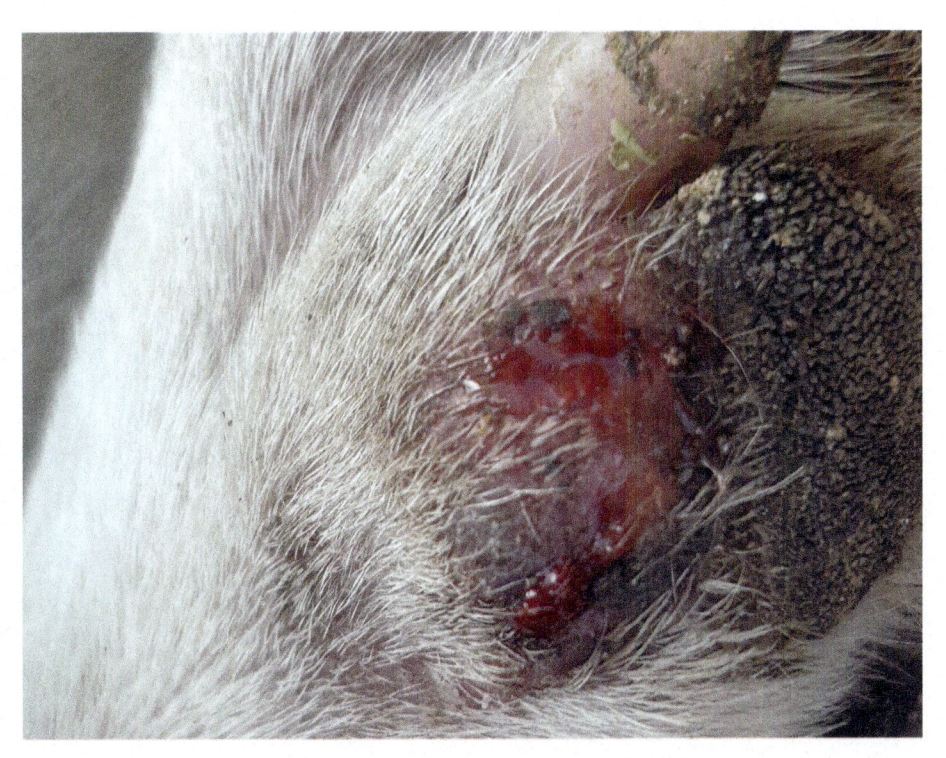

Sores on paws due to allergies

CHAPTER 7: TREATS, CHEWS, AND SUPPLEMENTS: ENHANCING YOUR BEST FRIEND'S DIET

The world of dog treats, chews, and supplements is a vast and often confusing landscape and as a dog care professional, I've seen firsthand the impact these extras can have on our canine companions, both positive and negative. This chapter aims to navigate this complex terrain, separating helpful additions from potentially harmful ones, and providing insights on how to truly enhance your dog's diet and overall well-being.

Let's start with a hard truth: many commercial treats contain ingredients that are far from ideal. Some added preservatives have been linked to serious health issues, including cancer and organ damage, and it's a sobering thought that we could potentially be harming our dogs in the long run. If you see long, unpronounceable chemical names, it might be best to look for alternatives.

Speaking of alternatives, nature provides us with some fantastic options that are both convenient and healthy. As well as carrots and apples (frozen or not) - which are wonderfully crunchy, and are packed with nutrients, as well as being low in calories and good for teething puppies - safer alternatives like antlers, backstrap, or tendon chews are natural options that are long-lasting and can help maintain dental health without the risks associated with some commercial products. Many popular dental chews fall short of their promises and while they claim to clean teeth and freshen breath, many are ineffective and may contain unnecessary, potentially harmful ingredients.

It's also crucial to mention the potential dangers of rawhide chews as despite their popularity, rawhides can pose serious risks, including choking and intestinal blockages. They're often processed with chemicals that you probably don't want your dog ingesting, so it's probably best to avoid these and opt for safer alternatives.

Now, let's talk about 'human food' treats. While sharing your food might seem like a loving gesture, it's important to exercise extreme caution. Foods like onions, garlic, chocolate, and even cheese can be toxic or harmful to dogs, so always do your research before giving any human food, and if in doubt, stick to dog-specific treats.

Here's a thought that might surprise you: treats aren't essential if dogs are fed a good, healthy diet. In fact, unnecessary treats are often a significant contributor to weight problems, especially when owners use treats excessively, either out of habit or as a way to manage behavioural issues. While positive reinforcement has its place in training, overreliance on treats can be counterproductive and lead to a host of other health problems.

The importance of not overfeeding cannot be overstated and obesity in dogs is a serious health issue that can lead to a myriad of problems, from joint issues to diabetes. Remember, showing love doesn't always have to involve food. A good belly rub or a fun game of fetch can be just as rewarding.

In conclusion, while treats and supplements can have their place in a dog's diet, they should be used wisely. The best treat you can give your dog is you! Your time, attention, and a well-balanced, nutritious diet. Remember, a healthy dog is a happy dog, and that's the ultimate goal of any caring pet owner.

Joint supplement

CHAPTER 8: THE POOP SCOOP: WHAT YOUR DOG'S WASTE IS TRYING TO TELL YOU!

Let's face it, as dog owners, we spend a lot of time dealing with our furry friends' waste. It's not the most glamorous part of pet ownership, but it's certainly one of the most informative. That's right, your dog's poop can tell you a lot about their health and nutrition. So, let's dive into the world of canine excrement and discover what those daily deposits are trying to tell us.

First things first, let's talk about the ideal poop. I know it sounds strange, but there really is such a thing as perfect poop. The ideal stool is firm, segmented, and easy to pick up. It should hold its shape when you scoop it, leaving little to no residue on the ground. This type of stool indicates that your dog's digestive system is working well and they're probably on a diet that suits them.

Now, let's consider consistency, perhaps the most important factor when assessing your dog's doings. Soft or watery stools are often a sign that something's not quite right, which could be a dietary issue, or might mean your dog ate something that didn't agree with them. It might even mean that their food isn't suitable for their digestive system, but alternatively, it could indicate an illness. If soft stools persist for more than a day or two, it's time to consult your vet.

On the other hand, very hard stools can be problematic too as they might indicate that your dog is dehydrated or not getting enough fibre in their diet. Hard stools can be difficult and uncomfortable for your dog to pass, potentially leading to constipation.

Colour is another important factor to consider and normal dog poop is usually chocolatey brown, so significant variations from this can be cause for concern. For instance, black, tarry stools could indicate bleeding in the upper digestive tract, while red streaks might suggest bleeding in the lower digestive tract or rectum.

Speaking of blood in the stool, this is something that always warrants urgent attention. While a small amount of blood can sometimes be caused by something as simple as straining too hard, it can also be an indicator of more serious problems, such as giardiasis, a parasitic infection that can cause severe diarrhoea.

I remember one particularly messy encounter with a dog suffering from giardiasis. I was grooming this poor pup, and let's just say things got very messy, very quickly. It was a stark reminder of how important it is to address digestive issues promptly, not only for the dog's health but also for the sanity of anyone tasked with cleaning up!

If your dog is producing an excessive amount of waste, it might be time to take a closer look at their diet, as dogs fed low-quality foods with lots of fillers can't use much of what they're eating, so it simply passes through their system. On the flip side, I've noticed that raw-fed dogs often produce smaller, firmer stools. This is because raw diets are typically more digestible, meaning more of the food is used by the body and less is excreted as waste.

Sometimes, you might notice something unusual in your dog's poop, like worms, which is gross, but it's important to keep an eye out for these unwelcome guests and if you spot worms in your dog's stool, they'll need deworming treatment right away.

Frequency of stools is also important and how often a dog poops can vary based on their size and diet, but what's most important is consistency. If your dog usually poops twice a day and suddenly starts going four or five times, or conversely, if they start going less frequently, it could be a sign that something's off.

Now, I have to share one of the craziest poop-related stories I've ever encountered. We had a Bernese Mountain Dog named Norman at the daycare and one day, his owner threw a toy squirrel in the air, and before anyone could react, Norman had swallowed it whole! We were all in shock, wondering what would happen next, but a couple of days later, Norman produced what I can only describe as a 'chocolate fountain', and lo and behold, out came the squirrel! It was a messy, smelly affair, but it taught us an important lesson: dogs will indeed eat just about anything, and what goes in must come out!

This incident highlights the importance of checking your dog's poop for foreign objects as you never know what they might have gotten into when you weren't looking! From toy squirrels to socks, I've seen it all come out the other end.

Different diets can have a significant impact on poop consistency and smell, and dogs on a high-quality, easily digestible diet often produce less smelly poop, whereas dogs eating foods with lots of fillers or those that don't agree with their digestive system might produce waste that could clear a room!

Here's a fun fact for you: some dogs, particularly Labradors, are prone to eating poop. Yes, you read that right. It's a behaviour called coprophagia, and while it's disgusting to us, it's not uncommon in the dog world, so if your dog is a poop-eater, it's worth discussing with your vet as it can sometimes indicate nutritional deficiencies or other health issues.

Sometimes, your vet might ask you to collect a stool sample for testing and this is usually done to check for parasites or other digestive issues. It's not the most pleasant task, but it's an important one, so always follow your vet's instructions carefully when collecting a sample.

The best kind of poop I have to say is frozen winter poop! As gross as it sounds, any dog owner who's had to clean up after their pet in the depths of winter will know what I'm talking about. When the temperature drops below freezing, dog poop freezes solid almost instantly and it's easy to pick up, doesn't smell, and doesn't leave a mess. It's the small victories that count, right?

But in all seriousness, paying attention to your dog's waste is an important part of being a responsible pet owner as it's often the first indicator of health issues, and catching problems early can make a big difference in treatment outcomes.

Remember, changes in your dog's poop can be caused by a variety of factors. Sometimes it's as simple as a dietary change or a stressful situation but as we wrap up this rather unusual chapter, I hope you've gained a new appreciation for the humble dog poop. The next time you're out on a walk, bag in hand, take a moment to really look at what you're picking up. Your dog's waste has a story to tell, all you have to do is listen (or in this case, look).

In the end, being attuned to your dog's digestive health is just another way of showing how much you care. It's not glamorous, it's often smelly, but it's an important part of keeping your furry friend healthy and happy. So, here's to happy, healthy dogs with perfect poops. May your bags always be strong, your aim always true, and your dog's digestive system always in top form!

Soft, no formation, not a good poo

Solid, firm, good formation, good poo

CHAPTER 9: CHOPPERS AND CHOW: DENTAL HEALTH AND NUTRITION

Close your eyes and imagine the perfect doggy smile. Glistening white teeth, fresh breath that doesn't make you recoil in horror, and healthy pink gums that don't bleed at the slightest touch. Sounds dreamy, right? But for many of our furry friends, this vision of dental perfection is just that, a dream.

In reality, countless dogs suffer from dental issues that can lead to pain, discomfort, and even serious health problems down the line, and as much as we might like to blame it on genetics or just plain old bad luck, the truth is that a lot of these issues stem from one key factor: diet.

As a dog groomer and daycare owner, I've seen my fair share of smiles, from the toothy grins of happy puppies to the more tentative smiles of older dogs who may be hiding some dental discomfort, but one thing I've learned over the years is that a healthy mouth is the foundation for a happy, healthy dog. Just like humans, a big part of maintaining those pearly whites comes down to what we put in our bodies.

Now, I know what you might be thinking, 'But dogs don't brush their teeth like we do! How important can dental health really be?' But, let me tell you, it's absolutely crucial. Just like humans, poor dental hygiene in dogs can lead to a whole host of problems, from bad breath and tooth loss to more serious issues like heart disease and kidney failure.

So, how can we keep our furry friends' choppers in tip-top shape? One of the best things you can do is offer your dog plenty of opportunities to chew. And no, I don't mean on your favourite pair of shoes or the leg of your antique dining table, I'm talking about safe, appropriate chews that not only satisfy your dog's natural urge to gnaw but also help to scrape away plaque and tartar build-up.

One option that many dog owners swear by is raw bones. Now, before you go tossing your pup a T-bone from last night's dinner, let me clarify, we're talking about raw, uncooked bones, ideally from a reputable source like a butcher or pet supply store. Cooked bones can splinter and cause all sorts of nasty problems, so it's best to steer clear of those.

When it comes to raw bones, size matters. You want to choose a bone that's large enough so that your dog can't just gulp it down whole but not so big that they can't get their mouth around it, and as with any chew, supervision is key. Keep an eye on your pup while they're gnawing away, and if the bone starts to splinter or break into small pieces, it's time to take it away and replace it with a fresh one.

Another fantastic option for dental health is definitely antlers, like the kind that come from deer and elk. Now, I know what you might be thinking, 'Won't antlers be too hard for my dog's teeth?' But the great thing about antlers is that they're naturally shed, so they're not as dense as other types of bone. They're also long-lasting, so your dog can chew on them for hours without wearing them down too quickly.

You can often find antlers at your local pet supply store, but if you're having trouble tracking them down, try asking your butcher. Many butchers work with hunters and may be able to source antlers for you, and if you're lucky enough to have a hunter in the family, even better! Just make sure the antlers are cleaned and free of any sharp edges before giving them to your furry friend.

I know that not every dog is a fan of chewing, and some may have dental issues that make it difficult or painful to gnaw on bones or antlers but that's where professional dental cleaning comes in. Just like we go to the dentist for regular cleanings and check-ups, our dogs need professional dental care too.

At Charlie's Place, we offer ultrasonic teeth cleaning for our furry clients which is a bit different from the kind of cleaning you might get at the vet's office as there's no anaesthesia involved, so the whole process is much quieter and less invasive. Instead of using traditional dental tools, we use a special ultrasonic scaler that vibrates at a high frequency to remove plaque and tartar build-up.

As ultrasonic cleaning doesn't make any noise or vibrate, so it's much less stressful for the dog and because there's no anaesthesia involved, there's no need for your pup to fast beforehand or recover afterwards. They can come in for their clean and be back to their normal routine in no time.

During the cleaning process, we use a special toothpaste that reacts with the ultrasonic scaler to create tiny bubbles and these bubbles help to blast away even the toughest build-up, getting into all those nooks and crannies that are hard to reach with a traditional toothbrush. Because the scaler vibrates at such a high frequency, it's also able to kill bacteria below the gum line, helping to prevent gum disease and other oral health issues.

You might be thinking, 'That sounds great, but how much does it cost?' And it's true, professional dental cleanings can be pricey, but when I took my own dog, Eric, to the vet for a dental cleaning a while back, it set me back a whopping £800, and that was just for a small dog. I can only imagine what it would cost for a larger breed.

At Charlie's Place, we believe that every dog deserves access to quality dental care, regardless of their size or their owner's budget, so that's why we offer ultrasonic cleanings for just £30 per session, which includes everything: the scaler, the toothpaste, and even a brand-new toothbrush head for each dog to ensure maximum hygiene.

Of course, even with regular cleanings, dental health starts at home and that's where diet comes in. Just like with humans, the food we feed our dogs can have a big impact on their oral health and a diet that's high in sugar and carbohydrates can contribute to plaque and tartar build-up, while a diet that's rich in whole, natural ingredients can help to keep teeth and gums healthy.

I know that raw feeding can be a controversial topic, and it's not right for every dog or every owner, but many proponents of raw feeding believe that the act of chewing and tearing through raw meat and bones helps to keep teeth clean and strong. If you do decide to go the raw route, it's important to do your research and work with a veterinarian or animal nutritionist to ensure that your dog is getting all the nutrients they need, and of course, always practice good food safety habits, like washing your hands thoroughly after handling raw meat.

Even if you don't feed raw, there are plenty of other ways to promote dental health through diet, so look for dog foods that are specifically formulated for oral health, with ingredients like enzymes and probiotics that can help to break down plaque and freshen breath, and don't forget about treats! There are plenty of dental chews on the market that are designed to scrape away build-up and keep teeth clean between brushings. Just make an informed choice.

Of course, no matter what you feed your dog, it's important to keep an eye on their oral health and watch for any signs of trouble as bad breath, excessive drooling, and reluctance to eat or chew can all be indicators of dental issues, so if you notice any of these symptoms, it's important to get your dog to the vet for a check-up as soon as possible.

Even if your dog's teeth are healthy, regular dental care is still important, and just like humans, dogs need to brush and floss daily and see the dentist every six months, as well as regular at-home care and professional cleanings to keep their choppers in top shape.

And that's where places like Charlie's Place come in handy. Our goal is to make dental care accessible and affordable for every dog, no matter what their size or breed and we believe that every dog deserves to have a healthy, happy mouth, so we're committed to helping owners achieve that goal. We know that dental health is about more than just clean teeth, it's about overall health and wellbeing, both for the dog and for their humans, and a dog with a healthy mouth is a dog who's more likely to want to play, cuddle, and show affection. And who doesn't want more of that in their life?

So, if you're a dog owner, I encourage you to make dental health a priority. Brush your dog's teeth daily if you can, or at least a few times a week, and offer safe, appropriate chews like raw bones or antlers, and don't forget about regular professional cleanings, whether at the vet's office or at a place like Charlie's Place.

Your dog's teeth may not be the first thing on your mind when you're snuggling on the couch or playing fetch in the park, but trust me, a healthy mouth is the foundation for a happy, healthy life. And as someone who's seen first-hand the difference that good dental care can make, I can tell you that it's worth every penny and every minute of effort.

So go ahead, give your dog a big, healthy smile, and remember, at Charlie's Place, we're always here to help keep those tails wagging and those choppers shining. Because at the end of the day, there's nothing quite like a happy dog, and a happy dog starts with a healthy mouth.

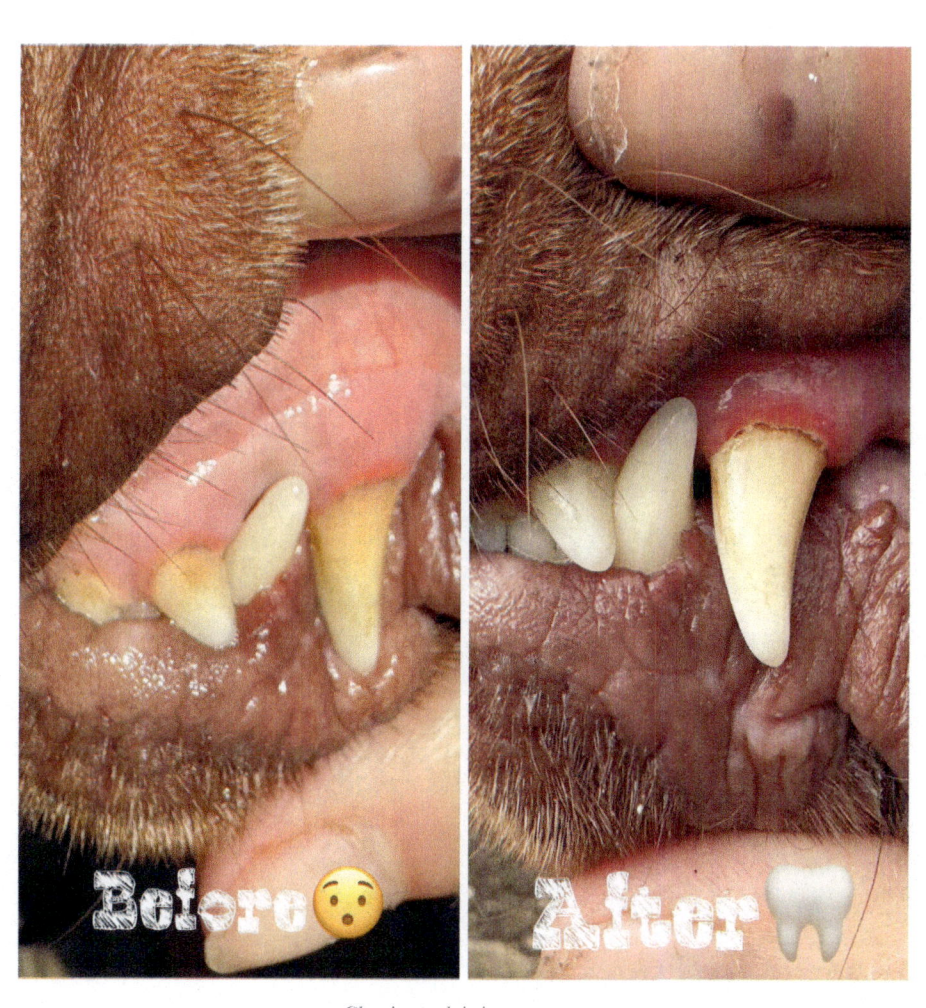

Cleaning teeth is important

Rabbit ears, best for flossing teeth

CHAPTER 10: BEYOND THE BOWL: EXERCISE, MENTAL STIMULATION, AND HOLISTIC HEALTH

When it comes to keeping our canine companions healthy and happy, nutrition is just one piece of the puzzle. While a balanced diet is undoubtedly crucial, it's not the only factor that contributes to our furry friends' overall well-being. To truly help our dogs thrive, we need to look beyond the bowl and consider the many elements that make up a holistic approach to canine care.

First and foremost, let's talk about the importance of exercise. Just like humans, dogs need regular physical activity to maintain a healthy weight, build strong muscles, and keep their cardiovascular system in tip-top shape, but not all dogs have the same exercise needs. It's essential to consider your dog's breed, age, and individual characteristics when developing an exercise plan.

Take huskies, for example. These magnificent dogs were bred to pull sleds across vast expanses of snowy terrain. They have seemingly endless reserves of energy and stamina, and they require plenty of opportunities to run, play, and explore. A quick walk around the block simply won't cut it for a husky as they need long, vigorous exercise sessions that allow them to stretch their legs and burn off that excess energy.

On the flip side, if you have an older dog or a breed that's prone to joint issues, like a bulldog or a basset hound, you'll need to take a gentler approach. These dogs still need exercise, but it should be low-impact and tailored to their individual needs. Swimming, for instance, is a fantastic way to provide a full-body workout without putting too much stress on the joints.

But exercise isn't just about physical health. It's also a crucial component of mental stimulation. Dogs are highly intelligent creatures with active minds, and they need plenty of opportunities to engage their brains. Without proper mental stimulation, dogs can become bored, anxious, and even destructive.

One of the best ways to provide mental stimulation is through interactive play, and this can be as simple as playing a game of fetch or tug-of-war, or as complex as setting up an obstacle course in your backyard. The key is to choose activities that challenge your dog's mind and keep them engaged.

Another fantastic option is puzzle toys. These clever devices are designed to make your dog work for their treats or kibble, providing a mental workout along with a tasty reward, and some puzzle toys require your dog to slide pieces around to reveal hidden treats, while others involve lifting flaps or spinning dials. The possibilities are endless, and there's a puzzle toy out there for every skill level.

WHAT NOT TO FEED YOUR DOG

Of course, mental stimulation doesn't have to involve fancy toys or elaborate games. Sometimes, the simplest things can provide a powerful cognitive workout. Take sniffing, for example. Dogs have an incredible sense of smell, and they love nothing more than exploring the world with their noses. By taking your dog on 'sniffari' walks, where they're allowed to stop and sniff to their heart's content, you're providing a natural form of mental stimulation that taps into their innate instincts.

But we should probably talk about the elephant in the room: overfeeding. As much as we love our dogs and want to shower them with affection, it's important to remember that excessive and unhealthy food is not love to a dog, as overfeeding can lead to a host of health problems, including obesity, joint issues, and even certain types of cancer.

The unfortunate truth is that canine obesity is a growing epidemic and according to recent studies, over half of all dogs in the United States alone are overweight or obese. This is a serious problem that can have far-reaching consequences for our furry friends' health and quality of life, so how can we combat this trend? The first step is to be mindful of how much we're feeding our dogs. It's important to measure out their food carefully and stick to the recommended serving sizes based on their age, weight, and activity level. Avoid free-feeding, which allows your dog to graze on food throughout the day, and instead establish a consistent feeding schedule with set meal times.

It's also crucial to choose high-quality dog food that meets your pup's nutritional needs without any unnecessary fillers or additives and to look for brands that use whole, natural ingredients like real meat, fruits, and vegetables. Avoid anything with 'by-product meal' or 'corn syrup' on the label, as these are often signs of a low-quality food.

But even the best diet won't do much good if your dog isn't getting enough exercise. Regular physical activity is essential for maintaining a healthy weight and preventing obesity, so aim for at least 30 minutes of moderate exercise per day; whether that's a brisk walk around your local area, a game of fetch in the backyard, or a swim in the local lake.

Of course, exercise needs can vary depending on your dog's breed, age, and individual characteristics and some dogs, like border collies, require more intense exercise to satisfy their high energy levels and working instincts, but others, like bulldogs, may need shorter, more frequent exercise sessions to accommodate their unique physical needs.

The key is to pay attention to your individual dog's needs and adjust their exercise routine accordingly. If your dog seems tired or sluggish, it may be a sign that they need more rest between workouts, but on the other hand, if they're bouncing off the walls with pent-up energy, it may be time to up the intensity or duration of their exercise.

But exercise and diet are just two pieces of the holistic health puzzle. Another crucial factor to consider is your dog's mental and emotional well-being. Just like us, dogs can experience stress, anxiety, and other emotional issues that can take a toll on their overall health, so one of the best ways to support your dog's mental health is through socialisation as dogs are social creatures by nature, and they thrive on interaction and connection with both humans and other dogs. By providing plenty of opportunities for socialisation, you can help your dog build confidence, develop important social skills, and form positive associations with the world around them.

This can include things like taking your dog to the dog park, enrolling them in a doggy daycare programme, or simply inviting friends and family over to meet your furry companion. The key is to expose your dog to a wide variety of people, places, and experiences in a safe and controlled way.

Another important aspect of socialisation is learning to read and interpret your dog's body language. Dogs communicate primarily through body language, and it's essential for both dogs and humans to understand these nonverbal cues. For example, a wagging tail doesn't always indicate a friendly dog. In fact, a high, stiff wag can be a sign of agitation or aggression, and similarly, a dog who is yawning, licking their lips, or turning their head away may be feeling anxious or overwhelmed in a particular situation.

By learning to read your dog's body language, you can better understand their emotional state and respond accordingly, which can help prevent misunderstandings, conflicts, and potential safety issues, both with other dogs and with humans.

But socialisation isn't the only way to support your dog's mental health, and another key factor is providing plenty of mental stimulation through things like the puzzle toys, training sessions, and interactive play. These activities help keep your dog's mind sharp, stave off boredom and destructive behaviour, and strengthen the bond between you and your furry friend.

When it comes to training, it's important to use positive reinforcement techniques that encourage your dog to make good choices and build their confidence, so avoid punishment-based methods, which can lead to fear, anxiety, and aggression, and instead focus on rewarding your dog for desired behaviours with treats, praise, and playtime.

Speaking of treats, it's important to use them sparingly in training and avoid overfeeding. While food rewards can be a powerful motivator, they should be small, low-calorie, and make up no more than 10% of your dog's daily caloric intake. You can also use a portion of your dog's regular kibble as training treats, as long as you subtract that amount from their daily meals.

Another important aspect of holistic health is regular veterinary care. Just like humans, dogs need routine check-ups, vaccinations, and preventive care to stay healthy and catch any potential issues early on, which includes things like annual exams, dental cleanings, and parasite prevention. Your vet can provide valuable guidance on nutrition, exercise, and behaviour, as well as help you navigate any health challenges that may arise throughout your dog's life, but vet visits aren't the only time you should be checking in on your dog's health.

Regular grooming is also an essential part of maintaining your pup's overall well-being. Not only does grooming help keep your dog's coat and skin healthy, but it also provides an opportunity for you to bond with your furry friend and check for any lumps, bumps, or other abnormalities that may require veterinary attention.

The frequency and type of grooming your dog needs will depend on their breed, coat type, and individual needs, but some dogs, like poodles and the bichon frisé, require regular haircuts to prevent matting and keep their coats looking tidy. Others, like huskies and German shepherds, have thick, double coats that need regular brushing to prevent tangles and control shedding. No matter what type of coat your dog has, it's important to use high-quality grooming tools and products that are specifically designed for dogs. Human shampoos and brushes can be too harsh for your pup's delicate skin and coat, so stick to products that are formulated for canine use.

In addition to coat care, regular grooming also includes things like nail trims, ear cleanings, and dental hygiene, and overgrown nails can cause discomfort and even lead to mobility issues, while dirty ears can trap moisture and lead to infections. As we discussed in the previous chapter, dental health is a crucial component of overall wellness, so regular brushing and professional cleanings are a must.

Another important aspect of canine health is hydration. Just like humans, dogs need plenty of fresh, clean water to stay healthy and function at their best, and this is especially important for dogs who eat a dry kibble diet, as they may not be getting as much moisture from their food as those who eat a wet or raw diet. To encourage your dog to drink more water, try placing multiple water bowls throughout your home and outside space, and you can even add a bit of low-sodium broth or wet food to make it more appealing. Just be sure to clean your dog's water bowls regularly to prevent the growth of bacteria and other nasties.

But hydration isn't just about water intake, it's also about maintaining healthy skin and a lustrous coat. Dry, flaky skin and a dull, brittle coat can be signs of dehydration, as well as other underlying health issues, so in addition to providing plenty of fresh water, you can support your dog's skin and coat health by feeding a high-quality diet rich in essential fatty acids, using a humidifier in dry environments, and avoiding harsh chemicals and excessive bathing.

Another factor to consider when it comes to canine health is the environment. Dogs are sensitive to temperature, humidity, and other environmental factors that can impact their comfort and safety, and hot weather can be particularly dangerous for many breeds of dog, as they don't sweat like humans do and can quickly overheat. When the temperature soars, it's important to provide plenty of shade, ventilation, and cool water for your pup, and to avoid strenuous exercise during the hottest parts of the day. You may also want to invest in a cooling mat or vest to help regulate your dog's body temperature.

Cold weather can also pose challenges for dogs, particularly those with short coats or low body fat, so when the mercury drops, make sure your pup has a warm, dry place to sleep, and consider using a coat or sweater to help them retain body heat. You may also need to adjust their exercise routine to avoid icy or snowy surfaces that can be hard on their paws.

WHAT NOT TO FEED YOUR DOG

Perhaps the most important factor however, in promoting canine health and happiness, is also the simplest: love and attention. Dogs are social creatures who thrive on interaction and affection from their human companions, and by providing plenty of love, playtime, and positive reinforcement, you can help your furry friend feel secure, confident, and valued.

Of course, this doesn't mean you have to be with your dog 24/7 or cater to their every whim, in fact, it's important to set clear boundaries and establish yourself as the leader of the pack, but this means providing structure, consistency, and positive discipline, and avoiding the temptation to treat your dog like a furry little human.

As much as we may anthropomorphise our dogs and ascribe human emotions and motivations to their behaviour, the truth is that they are fundamentally different from us. They have their own instincts, needs, and ways of communicating that are particular to their species and it pays to understand and love them for their own unique doggy nature.

By respecting and working with these differences, rather than trying to mould our dogs into something they're not, we can create a more harmonious and fulfilling relationship with our best friends; although this does mean taking the time to learn about canine behaviour, body language, and breed-specific needs, and adjusting our expectations and approach.

For example, a husky will never be content lying around the house all day, no matter how much we might want a low-maintenance lapdog, and a terrier will always have a high prey drive, no matter how much we might wish they'd stop chasing those pesky squirrels! A Labrador will always be prone to overeating, no matter how much we might want them to have more self-control, but by understanding and embracing these breed-specific quirks, we can provide our dogs with the right kind of exercise, mental stimulation, and training to help them thrive. We can also avoid setting ourselves up for frustration and disappointment by expecting them to be something they're not.

At the end of the day, the key to promoting canine health and happiness is to approach it holistically. This means looking beyond the food bowl and considering all the factors that contribute to our furry friends' physical, mental, and emotional well-being. It means providing a balanced diet, plenty of exercise and mental stimulation, regular veterinary care and grooming, and a whole lot of love and positive attention.

This may sound like a lot of work, and in some ways, it is. Caring for a dog is a big responsibility that requires time, effort, and dedication, but the rewards are more than worth it. By investing in our dogs' health and happiness, we not only improve their quality of life but also deepen the bond we share with them.

So, as we come to the end of this journey through the world of canine nutrition and holistic health, I encourage you to take a step back and look at the bigger picture. To see your dog not just as a pet or a possession, but as a beloved companion with their own unique needs, personality, and place in your life. Many people refer to themselves as dog mums and dads and I think this shows just how close we are and always have been. They really have become an important member of the family.

Above all, I encourage you to embrace the joy, laughter, and unconditional love that our furry friends bring to our lives; to savour the moments of connection and companionship, and to cherish the memories you make together. At the end of the day, that's what it's all about. Not the perfect diet or the most impressive tricks, but the simple, profound bond between a dog and their human. A bond that has endured for thousands of years and will continue to enrich our lives in countless ways.

So, here's to you and your furry friend. May your adventures be many, your love be boundless, and your dogs' tails always wag with joy.

Playing scent games is one of the best exercises for your dog

Agility

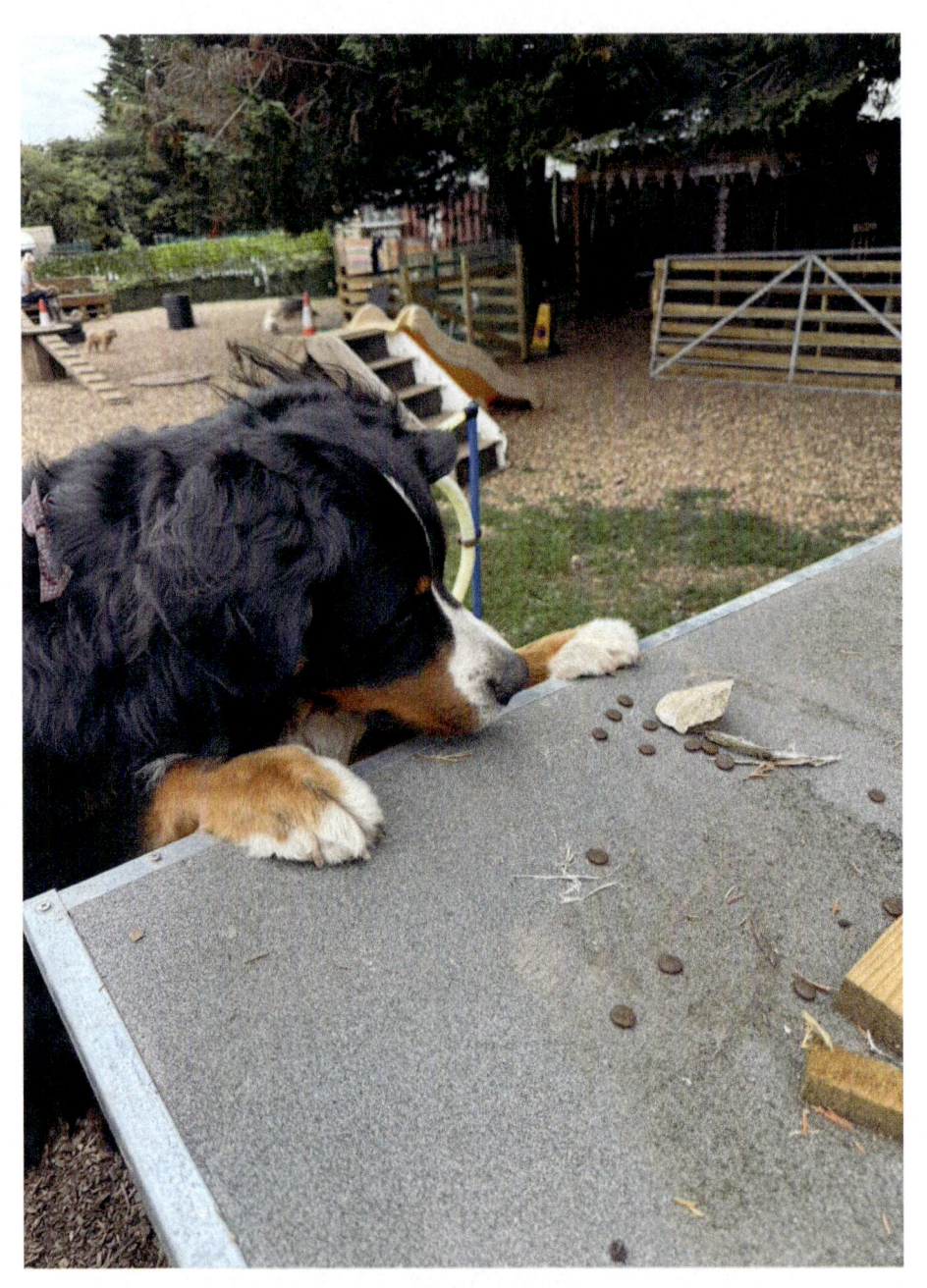

Find the treats

Hidden scents

Hidden balls with scents on

Printed in Great Britain
by Amazon